Gateaux & Pastries

DAVID & CHARLES
Newton Abbot London

British Library Cataloguing in Publication Data

Gateaux & Pastries.—(David & Charles Kitchen Workshop)
  1. Cake
  I. Dessertkaker. *English*
  641.8653   TX771

ISBN 0-7153-8463-5

© Illustrations: A/S Hjemmet 1980
Text: David & Charles 1983

Filmset by MS Filmsetting Ltd, Frome, Somerset
and printed in The Netherlands
by Smeets Offset BV, Weert
for David & Charles (Publishers) Limited
Brunel House, Newton Abbot, Devon

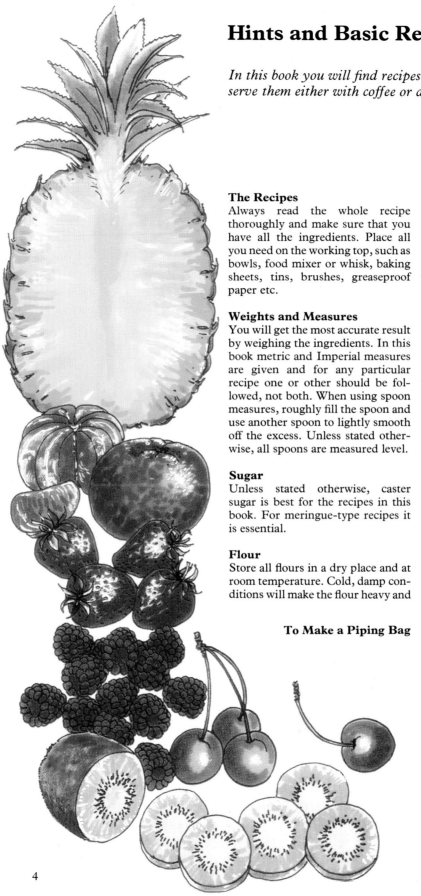

Hints and Basic Recipes

In this book you will find recipes for real luxury cakes. You can serve them either with coffee or as a dessert on festive occasions.

The Recipes
Always read the whole recipe thoroughly and make sure that you have all the ingredients. Place all you need on the working top, such as bowls, food mixer or whisk, baking sheets, tins, brushes, greaseproof paper etc.

Weights and Measures
You will get the most accurate result by weighing the ingredients. In this book metric and Imperial measures are given and for any particular recipe one or other should be followed, not both. When using spoon measures, roughly fill the spoon and use another spoon to lightly smooth off the excess. Unless stated otherwise, all spoons are measured level.

Sugar
Unless stated otherwise, caster sugar is best for the recipes in this book. For meringue-type recipes it is essential.

Flour
Store all flours in a dry place and at room temperature. Cold, damp conditions will make the flour heavy and full of lumps. This affects the baking quality. For a lighter result, always sift the flour. This will allow it to breathe and attain the right temperature.

Baking Powder (Soda)
This should be stored in a dry, but not too warm, place. The baking powder's rising ability starts the moment it comes in contact with flour and liquid. Mixtures containing baking powder should be baked as soon as possible.

Eggs
The recipes which follow use eggs weighing 65–70g (about 2½oz) each (Grade 2). Always use fresh eggs and take them out of the fridge at least 1 hr before you are going to use them. Surplus egg whites can be stored under cover for 4–5 days in the fridge. Egg yolks can be stored in the same way, covered with a little cold water.

Beating and Stirring
Traditionally, when making cakes containing fat, the beating to cream the butter and sugar and the ad-

To Make a Piping Bag

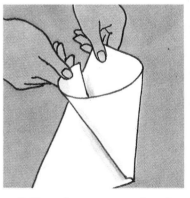

1 Fold one bottom corner of a triangular strong piece of paper up towards the top corner.

dition of other ingredients was done with a wooden spoon. An excellent result is also obtained by using a food mixer for blending the softened butter and sugar until it is white and then adding the eggs one at a time without stopping the mixer. The other ingredients are then mixed in by hand.

Alternatively you can put all the ingredients in the mixer bowl and blend for 1 min at the lowest speed and then $2\frac{1}{2}$–3 min at top speed. When using this method your cakes will not be as spongy as when using the 'old' method. Make sure you do not run the mixer for more than 4 min, otherwise the cake may collapse completely when you take it out of the oven.

Adding Dried Fruit etc
Chopped fruit, almonds, nuts and other similar cake additions should be mixed with some of the flour before being added to the mixture. The flour prevents them from sinking to the bottom while baking.

Rubbed-in Mixtures
Always use chilled butter and cut it into the flour by using a knife or crumble it in with your fingertips. When making pastry, it is very important that the room is not too hot, especially if there is a high proportion of butter in the dough. Even the heat from your hands can make this type of mixture sticky. Knead the dough only just long enough for it to bind together and appear smooth in consistency. Otherwise the end result may be tough and hard.

Sizes of Tins
Unless stated otherwise, the tins used in the recipes are 27cm ($10\frac{1}{2}$in) long loaf tins which hold $1\frac{1}{2}$ litres or $2\frac{1}{2}$pt (sufficient for about 1kg ($2\frac{1}{4}$lb) of mixture); round spring-form or loose-bottomed tins, 24cm ($9\frac{1}{2}$in) in diameter; and pie dishes 22cm ($8\frac{1}{2}$in) in diameter. The size of the larger Swiss roll tin is about 30×40cm ($11 \times 15\frac{1}{2}$in) and a small one (you can use the foil type) about 20×30cm (8×12in). If the tin you use has a larger diameter or is longer, you will not have enough mixture to fill it, consequently the baking time becomes shorter, and at a higher temperature.

In addition to the above mentioned standard baking tins, there are countless other variations: heart-shaped, in the form of numbers for birthdays, fluted, with holes and 'chimneys' in the middle. Take your pick, but remember the basic rules: deep tins – longer baking at a low temperature; shallow tins – shorter baking at a higher temperature.

Greasing of Tins
Melt butter or other fat in the tin, spread it over with a pastry brush and place tin in a cool place. Sprinkle with flour, finely sifted breadcrumbs or semolina. Shake off excess.

Greaseproof Paper
Use greaseproof paper on baking sheets and in large tins. This will make them easier to clean.

Baking
Switch on the oven well in advance and adjust to the right temperature. Unfortunately very few thermostats are accurate, so that it is wise to keep an eye on the cake in the oven, both as regards baking time and amount of heat. The baking times and temperatures listed in this book are, therefore, only a guideline. You will have to find out for yourself what suits your oven best. Testing to see if a large cake is baked through can be done by pricking it with a wooden cocktail stick. If this comes away without any dough sticking to it, the cake is ready. Small cakes should be golden in colour and, if pressed lightly with the finger, feel firm.

Cooling and Storing
All baked foods should be cooled on a wire rack, so that they do not end up having a soft and moist base. They should therefore be completely cold before you put them into airtight tins or deep freeze them. The recipes will tell you whether or not the cakes are suitable for the freezer. Use good quality plastic, tinfoil or specially made boxes (with lid) for the freezer. It is very important that you choose strong wrapping material. Cakes containing a lot of butter or other fat will keep in the freezer for about 2 months. Cakes containing meringue, jelly, mousse or cream fillings containing gelatine are unsuitable for the freezer, and already iced cakes must be treated with care or the icing may crack.

Defrost the cakes in their wrapping at room temperature. Decorate with icing or other decoration when they have thawed out.

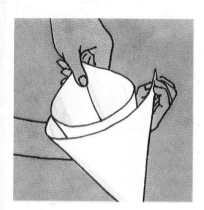

2 Grip with your thumb and twist the rest of the paper towards your thumb.

3 Fold the point inwards and fasten with either a paper clip or Sellotape.

4 Cut off the pointed end with a pair of scissors, making a hole suitable for the decoration you have in mind.

5

Hints for Fatless Cakes

● Assemble all the ingredients you are going to use beforehand.
● Do not leave the mixture standing, as the air will go out of it and the cake may not rise well.
● Whisk eggs and sugar until stiff.
● Sift in flour and baking powder.
● Pour the mixture into a greased tin and place in oven right away.
● Do not open the oven door too early. Changes in temperature can cause the cake to collapse.
● Cool cake for a while in the tin before you take it out.

Basic Sponge

Round baking tin, 20–22cm (8–8½in) in diameter
Preparation time: 15–20 min
Baking time: about 50 min
Oven temperature: 180°C, 350°F, Gas 4
Bottom rack in the oven
Suitable for the freezer

3 eggs, 225g (½lb) sugar
180g (6½oz) flour
2 × 5ml tsp (2tsp) baking powder
100ml (4fl oz) cold water

1 Whisk eggs and sugar until thick.
2 Sift flour and baking powder into the mixture, alternately with the water. Stir carefully.
3 Pour mixture into a well greased tin or tin lined with greased greaseproof paper. Bake as directed above.
4 Turn the tin carefully upside down and place on a wire rack. Leave cake to cool slightly before removing tin.

Large Sponge

Round baking tin, 26cm (10¼in) diameter
Preparation time: 15–20 min
Baking time: about 1 hr
Oven temperature: 180–200°C, 350–400°F, Gas 4–6
Place in oven on the bottom rack.
Use baking sheet, not grid
Suitable for the freezer

5 eggs
250g (9oz) sugar
100g (¼lb) arrowroot
100g (¼lb) flour
3 × 5ml tsp (3tsp) baking powder
3 × 15ml tbsp (3tbsp) cold water

1 Whisk eggs and sugar together very thoroughly in an electric mixer or with a rotary whisk. The mixture should be as stiff as possible.
2 Add the water and whisk thoroughly for a few seconds. Sift arrowroot and flour together with the baking powder into the mixture and run the food mixer at top speed for a few seconds, or whisk vigorously with the rotary whisk. Do not fold the flours in carefully.
3 Grease the baking tin, sprinkle well with flour and pour in mixture. Bake on bottom grid on a baking sheet for about 1 hr at a temperature of 180–200°C, 350–400°F, Gas 4–6. Do not open the oven door for the first 20 min. When cooked, allow cake to remain in oven with the door open for a couple of minutes before removing carefully from the oven. Leave to cool a little before taking it out of the tin.

Soft Sponge with Fat

Round baking tin 22cm (8½in) in diameter
Preparation time: 10–15 min
Baking time: 25 min
Oven temperature: 180°C, 350°F, Gas 4
Suitable for the freezer

150g (5oz) butter, 3 eggs
150g (5oz) sugar
150g (5oz) flour
1 × 5ml tsp (1tsp) baking powder
3 × 15ml tbsp (3tbsp) water or milk, coffee, juice or other liquid

1 Beat softened butter and sugar together until light and creamy. Fold in the eggs, one at a time, adding sifted flour and baking powder after each addition. Lightly stir in the liquid.
2 Pour into a well greased baking tin, and bake as directed above.
3 This sponge can be given various flavours – grated lemon rind, cocoa, chocolate, liqueur, ground almonds, chopped nuts etc.

Choux Pastry

Preparation time: 15 min
Baking time: about 20 min
Oven temperature: 200°C, 400°F, Gas 6
Suitable for the freezer

250ml (9fl oz) water
125g (4½oz) butter
125g (4½oz) plain flour
4 eggs

1 Boil water and butter and stir in flour until the mixture leaves the side of the saucepan and forms a ball. Cool slightly.
2 Add one egg at a time while stirring vigorously. The mixture is now ready for use as éclairs, choux buns or shaped into a ring. Further instructions are given in the relevant recipes.

Puff Pastry

Preparation time, including resting time for the dough: about 6 hr
Suitable for the freezer

250g (9oz) plain flour
150ml (¼pt) water
250g (9oz) butter

1 Mix flour and water to a smooth dough and leave in a cold place for at least 2 hr. Roll out to a rectangle.
2 Cut chilled butter into thin slices and cover two-thirds of the rolled out dough. (Use a cheese cutter if you like.) Fold over the third of the dough which is not covered with butter, then fold the last third with the butter on top over this. The pastry is now folded in three layers with butter 'facing' dough. Give a quarter turn. Roll out once again, fold as described above and seal edges by pressing with the rolling pin.
3 Leave the folded pastry in a cold place for at least 1 hr. Repeat rolling and folding 2–3 times with breaks of at least 1 hr between rollings and turning the dough a quarter anti-clockwise each time. Make a mark to indicate the right-hand edge each time you roll it out. Using and baking the pastry is described in the relevant recipes.
It is a time-consuming task to make this pastry, but unbaked it is suitable for the freezer. It can also be bought ready-made and frozen.

Shortcrust Pastry (Sweet) for Tarts and Flans Large Quantity

150g (5oz) butter
1–2ml tbsp (1–2tbsp) sugar
250g (9oz) plain flour
2 × 15ml tbsp (2tbsp) cold water and
1 egg OR 2 egg yolks OR
4 × 15ml tbsp (4tbsp) sour cream

This amount is sufficient to make a

flan base 22cm (8½in) in diameter with a lid or lattice on top.

Small Quantity

100g (¼lb) butter
1 × 15ml tbsp (1tbsp) sugar
150g (5oz) plain flour
1 × 15ml tbsp (1tbsp) cold water and
  ½ egg OR 1 egg yolk OR
  2 × 15ml tbsp (2tbsp) sour cream

This amount is sufficient to make a flan base 18–20cm (7–8in) in diameter.

1 Sift flour into a mixing bowl. Stir in the sugar. Cut butter into rough cubes and add to bowl. With finger-tips, very lightly rub butter into flour until the mixture resembles breadcrumbs.

2 Using a fork, beat the egg or egg yolks with the water just sufficiently to combine. Add this liquid, or the sour cream, to the flour and, with a knife, mix lightly until the mixture starts to bind together. Add a little more water or sour cream if necessary. Use hands to gently form the dough into a ball which leaves the sides of the bowl clean.

3 Roll out the dough on a board sprinkled with plain flour. Do not press the rolling pin too hard and roll out towards the edges, but not on the edge itself. Turn dough several times, but use as little flour as possible to avoid the pastry getting dry and hard.

4 Some flans are filled before they are baked, some are first cooked without their filling (baked blind) then, after the filling has been added, are put back into the oven to continue cooking.

Filled base
Baking time: about 20–30 min
Oven temperature: 200°C, 400°F, Gas 6
Lower part of oven

Empty base
Baking blind: 10–12 min
Oven temperature: 200°C, 400°F, Gas 6
Baking when filled: 8–10 min
Oven temperature: 220°C, 425°F, Gas 7

5 For special tarts you can use a pastry with more fat in it – up to 200–225g (7–8oz) butter, adjusting water if necessary. You can also add 25–50g (1–2oz) blanched, finely chopped almonds to the dough.

Party Gâteaux

1 Mandarin Gâteau
Make a Basic Sponge (see page 6) and cut it into two or three layers. Spread apple purée or jam mixed with whipped cream between the layers. Cover the cake with cream with a little vanilla sugar added and decorate with mandarin segments and toasted flaked almonds.

2 Gâteau with Berries
Make a Basic Sponge (see page 6), cut it into two, three or four layers. Fill with raspberries, blueberries (bilberries) and cream.

3 Nut Gâteau
Preparation time: 10 min
Baking time: 40 min
Oven temperature: 180°C, 350°F, Gas 4

150g (5oz) shelled nuts, 3 eggs
180g (6½oz) sugar
½ × 5ml tsp (½tsp) baking powder
1 small can of apricots

1 Grind the nuts and lightly mix together all ingredients. Pour the mixture into a small round tin, greased and sprinkled with breadcrumbs. Bake as directed. Slice sponge in two. Sprinkle cut surfaces with juice from the can of apricots and fill with chopped apricots. Decorate the top with cream and grated chocolate.

4 Lemon Gâteau
Make a Basic Sponge (see page 6) and slice it ·in two. Make Lemon Buttercream (see page 16), spread between layers. Cover with glacé icing, with lemon juice added. Decorate with candied orange peel.

5 Banana Gâteau
Make a chocolate cake following the recipe on page 19 and slice it in two. Sandwich layers together with whipped cream and sliced bananas. Decorate with cream and walnuts.

6 Strawberry Gâteau
Make a Basic Sponge (see page 6) and slice it in two. Sandwich together with strawberry mousse (see page 22). Cover the whole cake with strawberries and pour half-set strawberry jelly over. Make the jelly according to the recipe on page 28.

1 Slice the cooled sponge into two, three or four layers with a strong, thin piece of cotton thread or a sharp knife.

2 Stir liqueur or juice into the marmalade. Divide this and the buttercream evenly between the layers.

3 Cover the whole cake with buttercream and decorate with whirls, cocktail cherries and candied fruit.

Sponge with Chocolate Buttercream

Preparation time: 30 min
Baking: see Basic Sponge (page 6)
Settling time: 6–12 hr
Suitable for the freezer

1 quantity Basic Sponge (see page
   6)
Filling and Topping:
200g (7oz) butter
150g (5oz) icing sugar
2 × 15ml tbsp (2tbsp) cocoa
3 eggs
3 × 15ml tbsp (3tbsp) marmalade
1 × 15ml tbsp (1tbsp) liqueur
   (Grand Marnier) or orange juice
Decoration: candied orange peel or
   cocktail cherries, chocolate
   vermicelli

1 Bake sponge and leave to cool.
2 Make the buttercream by stirring softened butter until fluffy. Whisk the eggs and stir in icing sugar mixed with cocoa, a little at a time. Stir one spoonful of butter at a time into the egg mixture, making the cream smooth at each addition.
3 Slice, fill and decorate the cake as shown in the small illustration and large picture, mixing half the buttercream with orange marmalade and liqueur and using this portion of the cream for the top and sides. Leave the finished cake in a cold place for 6–12 hr before serving or freeze, either whole or sliced. The cake will keep in the freezer for about 2 months. To defrost, remove the wrapping, prise the pieces lightly apart and thaw for 3 hr at room temperature.

4 Wrap the cake in deep-freeze film. Place on a firm base. It will take 2–3 hr to freeze completely.

Cream cakes can be either simply or elaborately decorated. Above are some suggestions for decorating with almonds, fruit, jelly, chocolate pieces and whirls of cream – there are endless possibilities.

Liqueur Cake

Preparation time: 30–40 min
Baking time: see recipes, page 6
Settling time: 2–4 hr
Suitable for the freezer without glazing and decoration

1 quantity Basic Sponge or Soft Sponge with Fat (see page 6)
Filling: about 5 × 15ml tbsp (5tbsp) orange juice
6–8 × 15ml tbsp (6–8tbsp) liqueur or punch
75g (3oz) marzipan, grated
2 × 15ml tbsp (2tbsp) icing sugar
Decoration: 100–125g (4–4½oz) marzipan
150g (5oz) icing sugar
2 × 15ml tbsp (2tbsp) marmalade
2 × 15ml tbsp (2tbsp) lemon juice
50–75g (2–3oz) plain chocolate
50g (2oz) almonds, cocktail cherries angelica 'leaves'

1 Slice the cake into three layers. Spread the softened marzipan evenly over the base.

1 Bake the Basic Sponge or Soft Sponge with Fat. Leave until quite cold, then slice into three layers.
2 Make a smooth paste of chilled, grated marzipan, the tablespoonfuls of icing sugar and 2–3 × 15ml tbsp (2–3tbsp) liqueur or punch and spread this over the base.
3 Mix equal amounts, about 3 × 15ml tbsp (3tbsp), of liqueur and orange juice and sprinkle second layer with this.
4 Knead the marzipan for decoration with 50g (2oz) icing sugar and roll out into a round. Mix the marmalade well with 1–2 × 15ml tbsp (1–2tbsp) juice/liqueur and brush top and sides of the cake with this. Place almond paste layer on top.
5 Mix 100g (¼lb) icing sugar with the lemon juice and cover the top of the cake with this.
6 Sauté blanched, sliced almonds until golden in a dry frying pan and use to decorate the sides of the cake. Melt the chocolate in a basin placed in a pan of hot water. Pipe this onto cake, and arrange cherries and angelica, as shown in the illustrations.

Small Liqueur Cakes

Preparation time: 40 min
Baking time: 10–15 min
Oven temperature: 180°C, 350°F, Gas 4
Settling time: 2 hr or more

1 quantity Basic Sponge (see page 6)
Filling: 1 quantity Confectioner's Custard (see method)
Soaking: 50ml (2fl oz) liqueur and 50ml (2fl oz) water, mixed

Icing: 150g (5oz) icing sugar
about 2 × 15ml tbsp (2tbsp) liqueur cake colouring
Decoration: cocktail cherries

1 Make sponge mixture and spread it on greaseproof paper in a Swiss roll tin. Bake as directed above. Remove cake from the tin, peel off the paper and leave to cool on a wire rack.
2 Make Confectioner's Custard (see Chocolate Cake, page 14). Leave to cool.
3 Cut out small, round shapes from the sponge. Sprinkle half of them with liqueur mixed with water and leave to settle for 2 hr or more.
4 Divide the cream between the soaked shapes and place the remaining shapes on top.
5 Mix icing sugar and liqueur to a smooth, evenly blended icing. Add a dash of cake colouring. Cover cakes with icing, decorating each cake with a cocktail cherry. Leave in a cool place before serving.

This mouth-watering Liqueur Cake is now ready for serving! The 'spider's web' effect looks professional, but is easy to achieve.

2 Place the next layer on top and brush or spoon over with liquid. Place the third layer on top.

3 Brush sides and top with marmalade. Place marzipan, rolled out in advance, on top.

4 Make glacé icing and spread evenly over the surface, using a knife dipped in warm water.

5 Melt the chocolate in a basin in a pan of hot water, pour into a piping bag (see pages 4–5) and cut off corner.

6 Start decorating from the middle and pipe the chocolate to form a coil on the half-stiff icing.

7 Drag the chocolate out using a pointed knife, so that the top of the cake resembles a spider's web.

13

Chocolate-covered Cakes

Here are two tempting varieties – delicious either as dessert or with coffee.

Chocolate Marzipan Cake
Preparation time: 30–40 min
Baking time: see Basic Sponge (page 6)
Suitable for the freezer, if one is careful (the chocolate coating might crack)

1 quantity Basic Sponge (see page 6)
6 × 15ml tbsp (6tbsp) apricot purée
Confectioner's Custard: 2 egg yolks
2 × 15ml tbsp (2tbsp) sugar
1 × 15ml tbsp (1tbsp) cornflour
250ml (9fl oz) milk
a little vanilla essence
15g (½oz) powdered gelatine
250ml (9fl oz) double cream
Decoration: 200g (7oz) marzipan
150g (5oz) icing sugar
100g (¼lb) plain chocolate
20g (¾oz) butter
cocktail cherries, marzipan 'flowers'

1 Make the sponge and leave to cool.
2 Whisk egg yolks, sugar, cornflour, milk and vanilla over low heat until the cream is smooth. Stir in soaked gelatine. Continue to stir while cooling and, when cold, mix in the whipped cream.
3 Knead marzipan until smooth with the icing sugar and shape for top and sides. Melt chocolate and fat on low heat. Fill and decorate the cake as shown in illustrations.

Easy-to-make Chocolate Cake
Bake a Basic Sponge (see page 6), adding about 100g (¼lb) coarsely chopped plain chocolate to the mixture. Melt 100g (¼lb) plain chocolate with 20g (¾oz) butter on low heat and cover the whole cake with the icing as shown in the small illustrations on the left. Decorate with marzipan, nuts or pralines.

Right: Chocolate Marzipan Cake.
Top left: Easy-to-make Chocolate Cake.

1 Place the gelatine to soak in cold water, then allow it to melt in the warm vanilla cream, stirring constantly.

2 Slice sponge into three layers and place them on top of each other with apricot purée and vanilla cream in between.

3 Roll out just under half the marzipan to a circle for the top and the remainder into a strip to cover the sides.

4 Spread chocolate icing all over the cake. Allow this to stiffen and then decorate.

Almond Brittle Ring and Buttercream Fillings

This eye-catching ring filled with buttercream tastes as good as it looks. The examples of buttercream show how varied this type of filling can be.

Almond Brittle Ring

Preparation time: 30–40 min
Baking time: 30–35 min
Settling time: 6–12 hr
Suitable for the freezer, with or without decoration

*1 quantity Soft Sponge with Fat
(see page 6)
Buttercream: 250g (9oz) butter
250g (9oz) icing sugar
2 egg yolks
1 × 15ml tbsp (1tbsp) brandy
(optional)
Almond brittle:
150g (5oz) almonds
200g (7oz) sugar
1 × 5ml tsp (1tsp) butter
Decoration: cocktail cherries*

1 Grease a deep ring tin with melted butter and sprinkle with a thin layer of breadcrumbs.

2 Make the mixture following the recipe on page 6 and pour into tin. Bake for 30–35 min at a temperature of 180°C, 350°F, Gas 4. Use a wooden cocktail stick to see if the cake is baked through. Leave the cake in the ring tin for a short while before you take it out. Place on a wire rack to cool.
3 Beat the butter and icing sugar for the cream until soft and fold in the egg yolks. Add the brandy if used.
4 Blanch and finely chop the almonds. Melt the sugar in the butter in an iron frying pan or heavy saucepan. Stir in the almonds when the sugar turns golden brown, and turn off the heat so that the mixture does not burn. Continue stirring for a few minutes, then pour the hot almond brittle mixture onto a greased baking sheet. Crush when cold, using a rolling pin.
5 How to slice, fill and decorate the cake is shown in the illustrations below. The finished cake must be left in a cool place for 6–12 hr before serving.

Buttercreams
Chocolate Buttercream
Stir 100–125g (4–4½oz) softened butter with 50–75g (2–3oz) icing sugar, 1 × 15ml tbsp (1tbsp) instant coffee and 1 egg yolk. Melt 75g (3oz) plain chocolate on low heat, then cool to the same temperature as the butter mixture. Stir butter and chocolate together.

Nougat Buttercream
Stir 100g (4oz) softened butter with 100g (4oz) icing sugar. Add 50–75g (2–3oz) soft nougat, melted in a double saucepan or a basin standing in a pan of hot water.

Lemon Buttercream
Stir 100–125g (4–4½oz) softened butter with 100–150g (4–5oz) icing sugar. Stir in the finely grated rind of 1 washed lemon and add the juice a little at a time.

Orange Buttercream
This is made in the same way as Lemon Buttercream, but with 2–3 × 15ml tbsp (2–3tbsp) orange juice and the finely grated rind from ½–1 washed orange.

Sour-cream Buttercream
Stir 100–125g (4–4½oz) softened butter with 50g (2oz) icing sugar and 1 egg yolk. Stir in 100–150ml (4–5fl oz) sour double cream a little at a time.

French Buttercream
Boil 100g (¼lb) sugar and 3 × 15ml tbsp (3tbsp) water until it forms thin threads when lifted with a wooden spoon. Whisk 3 egg yolks until fluffy and pour the sugar mixture in a thin trickle into the eggs, while whisking vigorously. Continue to whisk until the mixture is nearly cold. Beat 200g (7oz) butter until soft and add the egg mixture, a little at a time. The cream will curdle easily if the egg mixture is too warm. If this happens, place the bowl in a pan of warm water (35°C, 95°F) and whisk vigorously.

Almond Brittle Ring
1 Pour mixture into well-greased ring tin sprinkled with breadcrumbs, and bake as stated.

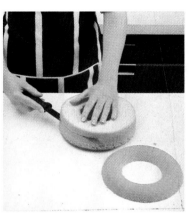

2 Slice the cooled cake in three or four layers with a sharp knife. Be careful when you get towards the middle.

3 Divide some of the buttercream evenly between each tier, making sure you take it out to both the inner and the outer circumferences.

4 Spread the rest of the buttercream on the surface of the cake until it is completely covered. Use either a palette knife or long ordinary knife.

5 Place crushed almond brittle on greaseproof paper. Toss over the cake.

Almond Brittle Ring is just as popular at teatime as with coffee. It is filling, so do not cut too large slices if you are serving it with other cakes.

Other Flavours

In addition to the already mentioned flavours, buttercream can be mixed with rum, liqueur, port wine, sherry, Madeira, brandy, fruit wine and fruit juice. Remember always to whisk or stir the liquid into the buttercream a little at a time.

You can also use dry flavourings such as cocoa, instant coffee, finely chopped almonds or other nuts, vanilla sugar, finely chopped candied or preserved fruit, crushed almond brittle, grated chocolate etc.

Chocolate Cakes

A chocolate cake of any description will always go down well – whether served as cake or with a glass of wine as dessert.

Brown Walnut Cake (above)
Preparation time: 15–20 min
Baking time: 45–55 min
Oven temperature: 180°C, 350°F, Gas 4
Bottom of the oven
Suitable for the freezer without cream and icing

100g (¼lb) plain chocolate
150g (5oz) butter, 3 eggs (separated)

175g (6oz) sugar
100g (¼lb) walnuts
1 × 5ml tsp (1tsp) instant coffee
200g (7oz) plain flour
2 × 5ml tsp (2tsp) baking powder
100ml (4fl oz) single cream
½ quantity Confectioner's Custard (see Chocolate Cake, page 14)
1 × 15ml tbsp (1tbsp) light port wine (optional)
Icing : 85–125g (3½–4½oz) icing sugar
1 × 5ml tsp (1tsp) instant coffee

1 Break the chocolate into pieces and place these in a bowl. Place the bowl in a pan of hot water, or on very low heat on the hot plate.
2 Beat butter with the sugar until light and fluffy and fold in the egg yolks one by one. Stir in the melted and cooled chocolate.
3 Put aside 8–10 walnut halves,

finely chop the rest and mix with instant coffee, plain flour and baking powder. Stir into the butter alternately with the cream. Whisk the egg whites until stiff and fold them in lightly. Pour mixture into a greased spring-form tin sprinkled with flour and bake as indicated above. Prick the cake with a wooden cocktail stick to test if it is baked through. Turn out on a wire rack to cool.
4 Add the port wine to the ½ quantity of Confectioner's Custard. Slice the cake into two, spread the Confectioner's Custard on one half and place the other half on top. Mix the icing sugar with the instant coffee and stir in hot water until the icing is smooth and of the correct consistency. Spread the icing over the cake and decorate with walnut halves.

Chocolate Cake with Cream
(above)
Preparation time: about 20 min
Baking time: 45–50 min
Oven temperature: 180°C, 350°F, Gas 4
Middle part of the oven
Unsuitable for the freezer

200g (7oz) butter
100g (¼lb) icing sugar
125g (4½oz) sugar
40g (1½oz) cocoa, 5 eggs
200g (7oz) plain flour
2 × 5ml tsp (2tsp) baking powder
Filling and decoration:
500ml (18fl oz) double cream
about 150ml (¼pt) apricot purée
grated chocolate

1 Mix softened butter with icing sugar, sugar and cocoa. Add the eggs, one at a time, stirring well between each addition. Sift plain flour and baking powder together and stir in.
2 Grease and flour a round tin and spoon in the mixture. Bake as indicated above. Leave to cool on a wire rack. Cut into four layers.
3 Whip the cream until stiff, but not dry. Mix in the apricot purée, adding a very little icing sugar if the cream is not sweet enough. Place the layers together with cream in between and spread top and side of the cake with cream. Decorate with grated chocolate. Chill cake until you are ready to serve it.

Coconut Cake with Chocolate and Apricots
Preparation time: 15 min
Baking time: about 30 min
Oven temperature: 180°C, 350°F, Gas 4

175g (6oz) desiccated coconut
3 egg whites
100g (4oz) sugar
50g (2oz) grated chocolate
Decoration:
250ml (9fl oz) double cream
small can of apricots
1 × 15ml tbsp (1tbsp) sugar
50g (2oz) grated chocolate

1 Whisk the egg whites until stiff and fold in the sugar. Carefully stir in the coconut and the grated chocolate.
2 Pour the mixture into a cake tin which has been greased and sprinkled with coconut. Bake as indicated.
3 Turn the cake out onto a dish and, when cool, decorate with whipped cream mixed with the sugar and chocolate. Place well-drained fruit in the middle. Serve immediately.

Swiss Rolls

Whether simply filled with jam or with a variety of fillings, they are always popular and are easy to make.

Light Swiss Roll
Preparation time: 20 min
Baking time: 8–10 min
Oven temperature: 200–220°C, 400–425°F, Gas 6–7
Middle of the oven
Suitable for the freezer

3 eggs, 100g (4oz) sugar
125g (4½oz) plain flour
½ × 5ml tsp (½tsp) baking powder
Filling:
jam, marmalade, fruit purée, fresh or frozen berries, cream or buttercream

1 Whisk eggs and sugar until very stiff. Sift in the plain flour mixed with baking powder. Stir carefully.
2 Make a paper shape slightly smaller than the Swiss roll tin (see illustrations below), or line the greased tin with greaseproof paper.
3 Spread the mixture evenly in the tin, leaving it a little thicker along the edges than in the middle.
4 Bake until lightly golden in preheated oven and turn out onto greaseproof paper sprinkled with sugar – mixed with finely chopped almonds or nuts (optional). Remove paper shape or greaseproof paper. Brush the paper with cold water if it

sticks to the cake.
5 Spread jam, marmalade, berries or fruit purée on top of the hot sponge and roll it up immediately. Leave to cool with the join facing down.
6 If you are going to fill the roll with whipped cream, ice cream or buttercream, this must be spread on when the sponge is cold. Place a moist paper or cloth on top of the sponge when cooling, otherwise it will be difficult to roll up.

Swiss Roll with Mousse
1 quantity Light Swiss Roll (this page)
1 quantity Cake Mousse (see page 22)

1 Bake the Swiss Roll and fill it with jam. Cool completely.
2 Make the mousse, using lemon juice as the flavouring.
3 Slice the Swiss Roll and arrange the slices in a round spring-form tin.
4 Pour mousse on top of slices and place the tin or bowl in a cold place.
5 Remove the tin and place the cake on a dish when the mousse is set.

Chocolate Swiss Roll
Make a mixture identical to the one used for Light Swiss Roll and add 2 × 15ml tbsp (2tbsp) cocoa to the flour/baking powder mixture. Bake as prescribed for Light Swiss Roll. Normally a Chocolate Swiss Roll is filled with buttercream, but orange marmalade or whipped cream with finely chopped nuts or banana slices will also give it a delicious flavour.

Ice cream, cream and fresh berries turn a Swiss Roll into a summery delight.

Swiss Roll filled with Ice Cream
Cream, and thin slices of vanilla ice cream are spread evenly on the cold cake. Roll up by means of the paper. Place the cake on a serving dish with the join facing down.

Paper Shape

1 Fold in 2–3cm (about 1in) along all sides of a sheet of greaseproof paper.

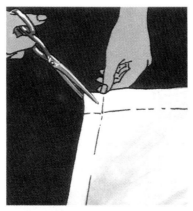

2 Carefully make a slit at an angle in each corner.

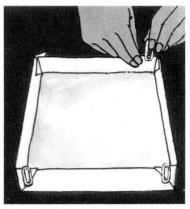

3 Turn up the edges and fold in the corners. Fasten with paper clips.

Filling a Swiss Roll

1 Turn out cake onto greaseproof paper sprinkled with sugar and pull off the paper shape.

2 Trim the edges if they appear hard, and spread the filling evenly over the cake surface.

3 Roll up the cake by means of the paper. Place the cake on dish with the join facing down.

The cake on the left has grated orange rind added to the basic mixture and is coated with icing sugar mixed with orange juice. Above right: Orange Cake with Mousse.

Cake Mousse
Preparation time: 20 min
Cooling time: 1–2 hr

20g (¾oz) powdered gelatine
2 eggs, 50–100g (2–4oz) sugar
100ml (4fl oz) liquid (fruit juice,
  wine, syrups from fruit, fruit
  purée, etc)
100–200ml (4–7fl oz) double cream

1 Soak the gelatine in cold water for about 10 min, squeeze off excess water. Melt in a bowl placed in a pan of hot water, or in 2–3 × 15ml tbsp (2–3tbsp) hot liquid.
2 Separate eggs. Whisk yolks and sugar until light and fluffy. Use more sugar for sour liquids, for instance lemon juice, than for juices from tinned or boiled fruit.

3 Stir the fruit or wine liquid into the egg mixture. Add melted gelatine by pouring thinly and stirring vigorously all the time. Leave until mixture starts to stiffen.
4 In separate bowls, whisk egg whites and cream until quite stiff. Fold alternately into the fruit and eggs. Pour the mousse over the cake base at once, and leave until completely set.

Orange Cake with Mousse
Preparation time: 30 min
Baking time: see recipes, page 6
Cooling and setting: about 2 hr
Unsuitable for the freezer

1 quantity Basic Sponge or Soft
  Sponge with Fat (see page 6)
mousse made with orange juice (see

previous recipe) ½ quantity Jelly
made with equal proportions of
sweet white wine and orange juice
(see page 28)
1–2 oranges

1 Bake the cake in a 20–22cm (8–8½in) spring-form tin and slice into two layers.
2 Wash, rinse and thoroughly dry the baking tin the sponge was cooked in. Place one of the layers back in the tin and pour mousse on top. Place the other layer on top of this and leave cake in a cold place for about 1 hr until the mousse has nearly set.
3 Slice 1–2 oranges into wedges and remove as much of the white and transparent membrane as possible. Arrange the wedges on the cake.

Pear Cake with Chocolate Coating. The same cake, sprinkled with flaked almonds, appears on the cover of this book.

4 Allow the $\frac{1}{2}$ portion of jelly to nearly set, then spoon it over the oranges. Leave the cake in a cold place for about 1 hr.

5 Loosen the cake from the tin by slipping a knife round the edge. Carefully remove the spring-form side, leaving the base.

Pear Cake with Chocolate Coating

Preparation time: 30 min
Baking time: 35–40 min
Oven temperature: 200°C, 400°F, Gas 6
Middle of the oven
Unsuitable for the freezer

1 large quantity of Shortcrust Pastry (see page 7)
Filling: 5–6 ripe pears, 175g (6oz)
sugar and 100ml (4fl oz) sweet white wine OR 1 large can of pears
100g ($\frac{1}{4}$lb) almonds, 2 eggs
100ml (4fl oz) double cream
$\frac{1}{2} \times 15$ml tbsp ($\frac{1}{2}$tbsp) plain flour
100–125g (4–4$\frac{1}{2}$oz) plain chocolate
1 × 15ml tbsp (1tbsp) butter
2–3 × 15ml tbsp (2–3tbsp) strong coffee
Decoration: 150ml ($\frac{1}{4}$pt) double cream
chopped nuts or almonds

1 Roll out the pastry and line a well greased and floured loose-bottomed flan tin 25cm (10in) in diameter.

2 Bring 75g (3oz) sugar, the white wine and 100ml (4fl oz) water to the boil. Add peeled, cored and halved pears. Simmer gently until barely tender and leave in the liquid until they are cold. If using canned pears, omit this step.

3 Blanch the almonds, grind them and stir in the eggs, the remaining sugar, cream, plain flour and 2 × 15ml tbsp (2tbsp) sugar syrup from the pears. Pour this mixture into the pastry base. Bake as directed, then cool.

4 Remove cake carefully from the tin, sprinkle surface with 1–2 × 15ml tbsp (1–2tbsp) sugar syrup and place well-drained pears on top.

5 Melt chocolate and butter in a bowl placed in a pan of hot water and stir in the coffee. Dry pears with a paper towel and spoon melted chocolate over the cake until it is completely covered. Place in a cold spot, but not in the fridge. Decorate with whipped cream and nuts.

Layer Upon Layer

Delight your guests with thin, delicious layers of cake filled or topped with cream and other temptations.

Almond Mocha Cake

Preparation time: 30 min
Baking time: 25–30 min
Oven temperature: 180°C, 350°F, Gas 4
Middle of the oven
Unsuitable for the freezer

1 quantity Fragilité (see page 29)
Filling : $\frac{1}{2}$ quantity French
  Buttercream (see page 16)
1 × 15ml tbsp (1tbsp) cocoa
1 × 15ml tbsp (1tbsp) instant coffee
350ml (12fl oz) double cream

1 Spread the mixture over the bottom of two identical, well greased and flour-sprinkled spring-form baking tins (or onto grease-proof paper).
Bake as directed and carefully place the cake on a wire rack to cool.
2 Whip the double cream until thick. Mix the French buttercream with cocoa and $\frac{1}{2}$–$\frac{3}{4}$ × 15ml tbsp ($\frac{1}{2}$–$\frac{3}{4}$tbsp) instant coffee. Place buttercream on one of the layers and cover with cream. Place the other layer on top, decorate with stiffly whipped cream and sift over the remaining instant coffee.

Layer Cake with Berries

Preparation time: 30 min
Baking time: 10–12 min
Oven temperature: 220°C, 425°F, Gas 7
Middle of the oven
Unfilled, it is suitable for the freezer

Layer Cake with Berries

1 Add one egg at a time. Stir well between each addition.
2 Spread the dough evenly in three circles on top of baking sheets sprinkled with flour, or onto greaseproof paper.
3 Spread one of the layers with some of the whipped cream.
4 Arrange berries evenly (reserving a few) and add more cream.
5 Place the second layer on top and spread over more cream. Decorate with the crumbled third layer, whirls of cream and a few more berries.

1

2

1 quantity Choux Pastry (see page 6)
Filling : 300–400g (about ¾lb) blackberries or other fresh or frozen berries
400–500ml (¾–1pt) double cream icing sugar, vanilla essence

1 Bake three layers of Choux Pastry (see step-by-step illustrations). Place two to cool on wire racks. Crumble the third with a fork the minute you take it out of the oven.
2 Fill as shown in the small illustrations. Add vanilla essence or icing sugar to taste to the cream before whipping.

Hints on Whipping Cream

● Use a bowl with a rounded bottom.
● Do not put too much cream in the bowl. Leave room for air above the whisk.
● If you are sweetening the cream, add the sugar before you start whipping. Fruit juices etc should be mixed into the cream after it is whipped.
● The cream you use for decoration must be completely stiff. A plastic or linen bag with a nozzle gives an excellent result. Do not grip the filled part of the bag, as your hands will heat the cream.
● Whipped cream should be stored well covered – preferably in the fridge. If you leave it for a long time, re-whip it as some of the cream will sink to the bottom.

Forget the calories and enjoy the flavour.
Left : Crisp Almond Mocha Cake.
Right : Layer Cake with Berries.

3

4 **5**

Strawberry-mousse Torte

Preparation time: 30 min
Baking time: 15–20 min
Oven temperature: 200°C, 400°F, Gas 6
Middle of the oven
Cooling and setting: about 2 hr
Unsuitable for the freezer

1 small quantity Shortcrust Pastry (see page 7)
1 quantity Cake Mousse with 100ml (4fl oz) strawberry purée (see page 22)
500g (about 1lb) fresh or frozen strawberries
2–3ml tbsp (2–3tbsp) sugar, ½ lemon
¼ quantity Jelly with strawberry flavour (see page 28)
250ml (9fl oz) double cream
10–12 almonds

1

2

1 Make the pastry and roll out thinly. Cut out the base as shown in the illustrations. Bake as indicated above. Place the baked pastry base in a cool place.
2 Cover the inside of the spring-form tin with double tinfoil.
3 Rinse and hull the strawberries and leave them in the sugar and the juice of ½ lemon for about 30 min. Use the syrup for the jelly.
4 Make the mousse with 100 ml (4fl oz) crushed berries. Spoon into the tin and allow to set.
5 Remove the baking-tin side and the tinfoil and decorate with whole or halved berries. Spoon over the half-set jelly. Leave in a cool place to finish setting.
6 Decorate this dessert cake with whipped cream and toasted flaked almonds.

VARIATION
Make a torte base following above recipe. Crush 2–3 pineapple rings and add to the mousse. The syrup from the tin should be used in the jelly. Decorate the torte with whole or sliced pineapple rings.

TIPS
Berries and Confectioner's Custard
Instead of mousse, the pastry base can be topped with 1 quantity of Confectioner's Custard (see Chocolate Cake, page 14) and the jelly be made from ½ packet jelly. Vary the berries and flavouring of the jelly to suit each other.

Strawberry-mousse Torte

1 Cut around the base of the baking tin to make sure the pastry will fit. Bake base as indicated in recipe and leave to cool.
2 Place double tinfoil as smoothly as possible round the inside of the tin. This will make it easier to get the mousse out of the tin in one piece.
3 Spoon the mousse into the tin and smooth the surface. Place in a cold place until the mousse is set.
4 Gently unclip the tin, carefully remove tinfoil, and slide the base onto a serving dish.
5 Cover the mousse with strawberries and brush or sprinkle half-set jelly on top. Place in a cold place to allow the jelly to finish setting.

3

4

5

Lemon Torte

Preparation time: 30 min
Baking time: about 15 min
Oven temperature: 220°C, 425°F,
Gas 7
Cooling time: 1–2 hr
Middle of the oven
Unsuitable for the freezer

½ quantity Puff Pastry (see page 7)
    or use bought frozen pastry
Filling: 2–3 apples, sugar
200ml 7fl oz) sweet white wine
1 lemon
1 quantity mousse with 100ml
    (4fl oz) juice from the apples (see
    Cake Mousse, page 22)
1 quantity Jelly with lemon (see
    separate recipe)

1 Roll out the pastry to cover the
bottom of a spring-form baking tin.
Make sure you rinse this in cold
water first. With a fork, prick holes
in the pastry as close together as
possible. Bake as indicated. Remove
from tin and leave to cool on a wire
rack.
2 Gently poach peeled apple
wedges in white wine with sugar to
taste. Strain through a colander, reserving wedges and juice.
3 Make a mousse with 100ml
(4fl oz) of the juice and make a jelly
with the juice of the lemon mixed
with apple juice and a little water.
4 Place the cold pastry base on a
dish and place the spring-form side
around it. Spread some of the
mousse on the pastry and place
apple wedges on top. Cover with the
remaining mousse and leave in a
cold place until the mousse is set.
5 Pour the half-set lemon jelly over
the torte and leave in a cold place for
about 1 hr. Remove the baking-tin
side carefully before serving.

Jelly for Cake Decoration

15g (½oz) powdered gelatine
250ml (9fl oz) liquid (sieved fruit
    juice, wine, sugar syrup from
    tinned fruit etc)

1 Dissolve the gelatine in a little
water over a saucepan of boiling
water. Do *not* allow gelatine to boil.
2 Stir the melted gelatine into the
fruit juice or other liquid, until
thoroughly blended in.

*Lemon Torte – a refreshing summer
cake which is always popular.*

3 Leave jelly until nearly set and either pour, spoon or brush it over the cake.
NOTE: Wine, or fruit juices with a strong flavour, can be diluted with a little water until you get the flavour you want. Sour fruit juice like lemon must be either sugared or diluted with sugar syrup. Make sure, however, that the jelly has a flavour suited to what you are serving it with.

Crisp Almond Cake (right)
Preparation time 20 min
Baking time: about 10 min
Oven temperature: 200°C, 400°F, Gas 6
Middle of the oven
Unsuitable for the freezer

150g (5oz) butter, 125g (4½oz) sugar
100g (¼lb) almonds
1 × 15ml tbsp (1tbsp) cream
about 50g (2oz) plain flour
400–500ml (¾–1pt) double cream

1 Stir softened butter and sugar to a fluffy cream. Blanch the almonds, chop them finely and stir into the butter. Add flour and enough cream to make a soft but workable dough.
2 Shape the dough evenly on well-greased, floured baking sheets into three or four rounds. The dough will tend to spread a little, but gather it into shape with a palette knife. Bake as indicated until the rounds are pale golden in colour.
3 Carefully loosen the rounds and place them on a wire rack to cool.
4 Sandwich the layers together with whipped cream, adding a little icing sugar or instant coffee, cocoa, liqueur, port wine etc.

Fragilité (illustrated on page 34)
Preparation time: 30 min
Baking time: about 30 min
Oven temperature: 140°C, 275°F, Gas 1
Middle of the oven
Unsuitable for the freezer

4 egg whites, 100g (¼lb) almonds
2 × 15ml tbsp (2tbsp) plain flour
175g (6oz) icing sugar
Cream: 2 egg whites
50g (2oz) icing sugar
100g (¼oz) butter
300–400ml (10–12fl oz) strong coffee

1 Blanch and finely chop the almonds. Whisk the 4 egg whites until stiff. Mix almonds, 175g (6oz) icing sugar and flour and fold carefully into the whites.
2 Make a shape from greaseproof paper, about 18 × 36cm (7 × 14in), fasten the corners with Sellotape or paper clips and brush with melted butter. Spread the mixture evenly in the shape, bake as indicated, and remove the paper when the cake has cooled slightly. Place on a wire rack.
3 Whisk the 2 egg whites and 50g (2oz) icing sugar in a strong-bottomed saucepan on low heat until the mixture is thick and lukewarm.
4 Beat softened butter until creamy and stir in cold coffee, a little at a time, until the mixture is smooth. Fold the egg-white mixture carefully into the butter.
5 Cut the cake across the middle and sandwich the two squares together with cream. Dust with icing sugar and slice with a sharp knife.

Truffle Cake
Preparation time: 15 min
Baking time: about 50 min
Oven temperature: 180°C, 350°F, Gas 4
Suitable for the freezer

125g (4½oz) butter
250g (9oz) sugar
1 egg, 150ml (¼pt) milk
60g (2½oz) plain chocolate
300g (11oz) flour
3 × 5ml tsp (3tsp) baking powder
Filling: 125g (4½oz) butter
60g (2½oz) plain chocolate
300g (11oz) icing sugar
1 egg, rum or rum essence

1 To make the cake, break the chocolate into pieces and melt in milk on low heat.
2 Beat butter and sugar well together. Add the egg.
3 Fold chocolate into the butter and sugar mixture and add the flour mixed with baking powder.
4 Spoon into a well-greased spring-form tin and bake as indicated. Leave to cool on a wire rack.
5 Melt the butter and the chocolate for the filling on low heat. Fold in icing sugar and lightly whisked egg. Stir until mixture is smooth. Add rum or rum essence to taste.
6 Slice the cake into three or four layers and sandwich them together with chocolate filling. Spread the rest of the filling over the top blended, if you like, with strong instant coffee.

Eclairs and Cream Puffs

There is no difficulty at all in making these melt-in-the-mouth pastries.

Choux Pastry

You will find the recipe for Choux Pastry on page 6. It can be placed in little heaps on a baking sheet covered in greaseproof paper using two dessert spoons, or be piped from a piping bag. Pipe fingers, raised round shapes or rings. If you want to make a large ring, it is best to pipe two layers one on top of the other. Do not have the shapes too close together, to allow for rising when cooking.

Baking

Preheat the oven to 220°C, 425°F, Gas 7. Place baking sheet in the middle of the oven and bake the pastries for 20 min. If they are becoming too brown, lower the heat to 160°C, 325°F, Gas 3. Do not open the oven door for the first 10 min. When you think the pastries are cooked, gently shake the baking tray. They should be crisp to touch and tend to move freely over the surface. Alternatively take one out and, if it keeps its shape without collapsing, the choux pastries are ready. Cool on a wire rack.

Filling Choux Pastries

Cooled choux pastries are either sliced all the way through or you just make a small incision in the side with a sharp knife or a pair of scissors. Fill before serving with one of the following suggestions:

Cream

Flavour it if you like with sugar-sprinkled berries, crushed macaroons, chopped or grated chocolate, crushed almond brittle etc.

Mocha Cream

Add icing sugar, powdered coffee or cocoa to the whipped cream.

Vanilla Cream

This is made from whipped cream mixed with 1–2 egg yolks whisked until stiff with 1 × 15ml tbsp (1tbsp) sugar and a little vanilla essence.

Confectioner's Custard (see Chocolate Cake recipe on page 14)

Add vanilla essence, fruit juice, liqueur, rum etc to the cream.

Ice Cream and Mousse

Divide ice cream into slices or cubes; for Cake Mousse see page 22.

Icing-sugar Coatings

Stir sifted icing sugar with hot water, orange or lemon juice, strong coffee, rum, liqueur or other liquid until a thick, creamy consistency is obtained.

A stiffer white icing is made from icing sugar stirred into lightly whisked egg whites. You can also add cocoa, powdered coffee, ground almonds, chopped nuts or other ingredients to the icing sugar.

Chocolate for Coating

Melt chocolate on low heat. Spread onto the choux pastries with a butter knife, or pipe it using a piping bag with a thin nozzle. For want of anything better you can use a plastic bag. Cut a *small* hole in the corner and squeeze gently.

Classic Cakes

Cake à la Rubinstein
Preparation time: 1 hr
Baking time: about 15 min
Oven temperature: 150°C, 300°F,
Gas 2
Middle of the oven
Unsuitable for the freezer

Macaroon base : 100g (¼lb) ground
   almonds
2 egg whites, 100g (¼lb) sugar
¼ × 5ml tsp (¼tsp) bicarbonate of
   soda
Choux Pastry : ½ *quantity (page 6)*
Filling and decoration :
50ml (2fl oz) rum, and for
   sprinkling
100g (¼lb) raspberry jam
50g (2oz) melted chocolate
1 quantity Cake Mousse (page 22)
4 × 15ml tbsp (4tbsp) sugar
25g (1oz) almonds, chopped
1 × 5ml tsp (1tsp) butter

1 Mix ground almonds, egg whites
and sugar in a saucepan and stir
until mixture is smooth. Blend bicarbonate of soda with 2 × 5ml tsp
(2tsp) water and add to the ground
almond mixture. Spread the macaroon evenly on greaseproof paper, in
a circle about 20cm (8in) in diameter. Bake as directed.
2 Make choux pastry and place in
small rounds on a baking sheet covered with greaseproof paper. Bake
at 200°C, 400°F, Gas 6 for about
15 min. Cool, and coat with melted
chocolate.
3 Sprinkle macaroon base with rum
and spread raspberry jam on top.
4 Make the rum-flavoured Cake
Mousse, using the 50ml (2fl oz) rum
instead of fruit juice. When half set,
spoon the mousse onto the macaroon base in an even layer and place
the choux puffs around the edge.
5 Melt sugar in the butter in a dry
iron frying pan and, when the sugar
is lightly brown in colour, stir in the
chopped almonds. Pour mixture
onto a sheet greased with oil, cool
and crush. Sprinkle this almond
brittle over the cake.

Top left : Cake à la Rubinstein.
Bottom left : Sachertorte.

Macaroon Rings (page 42) can be served as above, filled with Cake Mousse
(page 22) flavoured with chocolate, coffee, rum or brandy.

Sachertorte (Chocolate Cake)
Preparation time: 30–40 min
Baking time: 1–1¼ hr
Oven temperature: 150–160°C,
300–325°F, Gas 2–3
Bottom of the oven
Suitable for the freezer

Sponge : 125g (4½oz) *chocolate,*
   preferably bitter
150g (5oz) butter, 175g (6oz) sugar
100g (¼lb) flour
100g (¼lb) blanched almonds, finely
   chopped
6 eggs, separated
Coating :
200–300g (7–11oz) apricot jam
Icing :
100–150g (4–5oz) plain chocolate
25g (1oz) butter

1 Melt chocolate for sponge on very
low heat. Cream the butter. Whisk
egg yolks and sugar to a thick consistency. When chocolate has cooled
to the same temperature as the
butter, fold it in until thoroughly
blended. Beat in egg mixture and
stir in the flour and almonds. Whisk
the egg whites until stiff peaks
form and fold them carefully into the mixture with a metal spoon until evenly
blended, a half at a time.
2 Bake the cake as indicated, in a
well greased spring-form tin. Cool
tin on a wire rack, then remove side
of tin to cool cake completely.
3 Cut cake in half horizontally.
Sandwich the layers together and
coat top and sides with apricot jam.
Leave in a cool place overnight.
4 Melt chocolate and butter on very
low heat and, using a knife, coat the
top and sides of the cake with the
icing. Put the cake in a cool place,
but not in the fridge, until the
chocolate is hard and you are ready
to serve it.

Left: Delicate French Waffles and (foreground) Fragilité (page 29). Right: Mille-feuilles Cake.

sugar and cornflour in a saucepan with thick bottom on a low heat until thick and smooth in consistency. On no account boil. Stir while cooling and flavour with the brandy. Whip the double cream until stiff and stir into the cooked cream.

4 Sandwich the waffles together with cream just before serving. French waffles without cream can be stored in airtight tins.

Mille-feuilles Cake
Preparation time: 30 min
Baking time: 12–15 min
Oven temperature: 220–230°C, 425–450°F, Gas 7–8
Middle of the oven
Unbaked pastry is suitable for the freezer

1 quantity Puff Pastry (see page 7)
1 quantity Confectioner's Custard as for French Waffles (above)
50–75g (2–3oz) almonds
icing sugar, apricot jam

1 Roll out the pastry until fairly thin and cut out 3–4 rounds about 20cm (8in) in diameter.
2 Place rounds on a baking sheet rinsed in cold water or lined with greaseproof paper. Bake until lightly golden and place carefully on a wire rack to cool.
3 Blanch the almonds, slice about one third into flakes and coarsely chop the rest. Sauté almonds until golden in a dry frying pan.
4 Place pastry rounds on top of each other with the cream in between. Spread slightly warmed apricot jam gently over the sides and carefully press on chopped almonds. Dust the top heavily with icing sugar and sprinkle with the almond flakes.

VARIATION
Gâteau Napoleon
Bake thinly rolled out pastry on rectangular baking sheets. Place the pieces on top of each other with Confectioner's Custard in between and ice the top of the cake with sifted icing sugar stirred to a thick consistency with a little raw egg white. Slice the cake with a serrated knife when the icing is hard.

French Waffles
Preparation time: 20 min
Baking time: 10–12 min
Oven temperature: 230–240°C, 450–475°F, Gas 8–9
Middle of the oven
Unbaked pastry suitable for the freezer

1 quantity Puff Pastry (see page 7)
about 200g (7oz) sugar crystals
Cream: Buttercream (see page 16) or Confectioner's Custard made from
3 egg yolks, 250ml (9fl oz) milk
2 × 15ml tbsp (2tbsp) sugar

2 × 15ml tbsp (2tbsp) cornflour
1–2 × 15ml tbsp (2tbsp) brandy
100–200ml (4–7fl oz) double cream

1 Roll out the pastry fairly thinly and cut out rounds using a 6–8cm (2½–3in) cutter. Sprinkle sugar crystals on the table, place rounds on top and roll until oval in shape.
2 Place the ovals, sugared-side down, on a cold baking sheet moistened with cold water, or lined with greaseproof paper. Prick cakes well with a fork and bake until lightly golden. Place on a wire rack to cool.
3 Whisk egg yolks with the milk,

34

Tartlets and Medallions

Small, delicate tarts filled with fruit topped with a whirl of cream and hey presto – a delicious dessert. Prepared in advance, they take only minutes to complete.

Fruit Tartlets

1 Rolled out pastry is cut into small circles by means of a glass or pastry cutter to a size to fit the patty tins.

2 Sheet patty tins are shown but you can, of course, use separate ones.

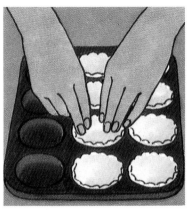

Fruit Tartlets (right)
Preparation time: 30 min
Baking time: 8–10 min
Oven temperature: 200–220°C, 400–425°F, Gas 6–7
Middle of the oven
Unbaked pastry can be frozen

1 quantity Rich Shortcrust Pastry with almonds (see page 45)
1 quantity Confectioner's Custard (see Chocolate Cake on page 14)
Filling : fresh, frozen or lightly stewed fruit
½ quantity Jelly made with sweet white wine and fruit juice (page 28)
Decoration : whipped cream, nuts, cocoa, chocolate, instant coffee etc

1 Roll out the pastry until fairly thin. Lift it up by the rolling pin and place across greased, flour-sprinkled large patty tins placed close together.
Roll the pin across the tins, so that a round of pastry falls into each hollow. Or you can use the method shown in the small illustrations, where the pastry is stamped out into 16–20 circles using either a glass or a pastry cutter, then placed in the patty tins.
2 Prick the pastry with a fork and bake until golden. Tap lightly on the tins to loosen the tarts. Place carefully on a wire rack.
3 Fill tartlets just before serving with Confectioner's Custard and fruit to taste. Spoon or brush half-set fruit jelly over the tarts and decorate with whipped cream and almonds, or other decoration.
The pastry tarts should be stored in an airtight tin for filling when needed. Sweetened fruit purée or jam can also be used as filling.

Medallions (right background)
½ quantity Shortcrust Pastry (see page 7) with 50–100g (2–4oz) finely ground almonds or other nuts added
apricot marmalade

1 Roll out pastry thinly and cut out rounds. Cut a whole in the centre of half of them.
2 Bake at 180–200°C, 350–400°F, Gas 4–6 for about 8–10 min, until light brown.
3 Sandwich together in pairs, with a thin layer of apricot marmalade between. Sprinkle with icing sugar.

Cones and Horns

Cream Horns

Roll out Puff Pastry (see page 7 or use bought frozen) until it measures about 20 × 30cm (8 × 12in). Cut into 10–12 strips and brush them with water. Twirl the strips carefully around the tinfoil cones with the brushed side next to the cone (see small illustrations). Brush horns with milk and sprinkle with sugar crystals. Place on a sheet covered in greaseproof paper or rinsed in cold water. Bake in the middle of the oven for 10–12 min at a temperature of 220°C, 425°F, Gas 7. Leave to cool, remove the tinfoil and fill with whipped cream.

Cones (1) (right)

about 20 cones
Preparation time: 20 min
Baking time: 4–5 min
Oven temperature: 220°C, 425°F, Gas 7
Middle or top of the oven
Store in airtight tins

100g (¼lb) butter, 100g (¼lb) icing sugar
100g (¼lb) plain flour
2 egg whites

1 Beat softened butter with the icing sugar until fluffy. Whisk the egg whites until creamy peaks form and fold into the butter mixture. Sift in the flour and mix until smooth.
2 Spread the mixture in thin rounds on greaseproof paper or greased, flour-sprinkled baking sheets. Bake as directed until lightly golden. Loosen cakes, one at a time, and twirl immediately into cones, either around the fingers or using specially made shapes. You can also shape them round a slim bottle.
3 Place the cones in a glass to cool. This way they will keep their shape. If the last ones go too stiff before shaping, place the baking sheet back in the oven for a short time. Fill the cones with whipped cream. Decorate with chopped cherries and grated chocolate (optional).

Cones (2)

Whisk 2 whole eggs well with 100g (¼lb) sugar, adding it a little at a time. Add 2 × 15ml tbsp (2tbsp) water and carefully mix in 100g (¼lb) sifted flour. Bake as above.

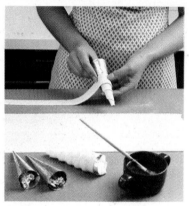

Pastry Horns

1 Cut strong tinfoil into circles 22–24cm (8½–9½in) in diameter. Cut in half and roll up the half circles in the shape of a cone. Place crumpled tinfoil inside.

2 Start rolling the strips of dough round the tinfoil horns, from the tip upwards. Make sure the strips overlap each other so that there are no gaps.

Light and Delicious

Cream Rolls

Use the same method as for the horns on page 39, but twirl around a metal stick or a roll of tinfoil. Carrots of even thickness make excellent shapers!

Remember to rinse shapers and baking sheets with cold water. The cooled rolls are filled with whipped cream. Sprinkling them with icing sugar adds a nice touch.

French Waffles

Use recipe on page 34. Place the waffles together in twos, with buttercream (see page 16) between.

Apricot Fluffs

Roll out Puff Pastry (see page 7) and, with a plain cutter, cut out rounds about 5–6cm (2–2½in). Put half of them on a baking sheet moistened with cold water or lined with greaseproof paper and brush the tops with a little raw egg white. Place 1 × 5ml tsp (1tsp) apricot jam on each brushed round and place the unbrushed rounds on top of this. Press firmly together and brush the surface with egg yolk. Remember to avoid touching the edges as this will prevent the pastry from rising. Place in a cool place for about 15 min, then bake at 220–230°C, 425°F, Gas 7–8 until lightly golden.

Small Puff or Shortcrust Pastries

Roll out Puff Pastry (see page 7) or use bought frozen pastry. Alternatively make Shortcrust Pastry, following the recipe on page 7. Roll out the dough to a rectangle. Cut out rounds with a plain cutter or a glass somewhat larger than the patty tins. If you are using shortcrust pastry, rinse the tins in cold water. When using puff pastry, grease the tins well and sprinkle with flour. Press the pastry firmly into the tins, prick with a fork and bake in the middle of the oven for 8–10 min at 220°C, 425°F, Gas 7. Turn the pastries out and cool on a wire rack.

Apricot Fluffs (at the back), French Waffles (in the middle) and Cream Rolls (in the front). These are all made from puff pastry.

Suggestions for Fillings: Raspberry Foam

Soak 15g (½oz) powdered gelatine in cold water for 10 min, then melt in a bowl placed in saucepan containing hot water. Mash about 350g (¾lb) raspberries, keeping some aside for decoration. Add sugar to taste and stir in melted gelatine. Whip 300–400ml (½–¾pt) cream, mix most of it with the mashed raspberries and use this mixture to fill the cases. When the filling is set, decorate with cream and raspberries.

Raspberry Foam will have a special flavour if made from wild raspberries – the flavour of summer and sunshine.

Nut Cream

Take ½ quantity Confectioner's Custard (see page 14) and add 50–100g (2–4oz) crushed Almond Brittle (see page 16). Carefully mix in 100–200ml (4–7fl oz) whipped cream. Fill cases with the cream and decorate with whole nuts.

Little Fancy Cakes

Petit Fours – basic recipe

200g (7oz) butter, 200g (7oz) sugar
3 eggs, 200g (7oz) flour

1 Beat softened butter with sugar and add the eggs, one at a time.
2 Stir in the flour and spread the mixture out in a small, well-greased Swiss roll tin measuring about 20 × 30cm (8 × 12in).
3 Bake at a temperature of 200°C, 400°F, Gas 6 for about 20 min and turn out onto a paper sprinkled with sugar to cool.

Petit Fours with Cherries

1 quantity basic mixture
100g (¼lb) butter, 1 egg yolk
100g (¼lb) icing sugar
1–2 × 15ml tbsp (1–2tbsp) liqueur

1 Make and bake the basic mixture and cut out small round cakes.
2 Stir butter and icing sugar well together, then add the egg yolk and liqueur to taste.
3 Place the small cakes on top of each other in three layers and put buttercream between. Decorate with cherries and glacé icing.

Chocolate Petit Fours

1 quantity basic mixture
about 200g (7oz) softened nougat
1 × 15ml tbsp (1tbsp) double cream
100–150g (4–5oz) plain chocolate
about 100g (¼lb) halved walnuts

1 Bake the basic mixture and cut out small round cakes.
2 Stir softened nougat with cream. Place the cakes in three layers with cream between.
3 Melt the chocolate in a bowl placed in a saucepan containing boiling water. Spread over the cakes. Top with walnut halves before the chocolate hardens.

Apricot Petit Fours

1 quantity basic mixture
100–150g (4–5oz) thick apricot purée
about 100g (4oz) marzipan
about 100g (¼lb) halved walnuts

1 Bake the basic mixture and cut out small round cakes. Place them on top of each other in twos with most of the apricot purée between.
2 Roll out the marzipan thinly and cut out small 'lids'.
3 Brush apricot purée over the top of the cakes and cover with the marzipan lids. Decorate with walnuts.

Easy-to-make Macaroon Dough (basic recipe)

Baking time: 5–6 min
Oven temperature: 220–240°C, 425–475°F, Gas 7–9
Use either the middle or the top half of the oven

500g (1lb 2oz) marzipan
125g (4½oz) icing sugar
1–2 egg whites

1 Knead the ingredients together in a thick-bottomed saucepan. Place on low heat and stir until mixture is hot (40–45°C, 105–112°F), firm, and smooth.
2 Leave to cool for a while and shape the dough as explained in the respective recipes. If you wish the mixture to be soft for piping directly onto a baking sheet, add more egg white.

Macaroon Rings

1 quantity Macaroon Dough
icing sugar, egg white

1 Roll the dough by hand into long rolls of finger thickness and squeeze them to obtain a triangular shape.
2 Slice the dough into 5–6cm (2–2½in) long pieces and shape these into rings. Pinch the rings with your fingers to make them look like five-pointed stars.
3 Bake, and cool on a wire rack.
4 Make an icing of icing sugar and egg whites. Drizzle over in thin stripes, using a piping bag with a writing nozzle.

Little Macaroon Cakes

1 quantity Macaroon Dough (see Easy-to-make Macaroon)
icing sugar, nuts, cocktail cherries, candied fruit or other decoration

1 Pour the soft macaroon into a piping bag with a large, star-shaped nozzle. Pipe small mounds directly onto a greased baking sheet or into small greased patty tins. Top with nuts, if used.
2 Bake at 220°C, 425°F, Gas 7 for about 5–6 min, then leave to cool. Decorate with glacé icing, candied fruit or other form of decoration.

Fork Cakes

1 quantity Macaroon Dough
5–6 × 15ml tbsp (5–6tbsp) icing sugar
about 150g (5oz) halved walnuts

1 Roll out the dough to a small rectangle, using icing sugar on the board when rolling. Cut out small round cakes and place on a baking sheet. Make lines on the surface with a fork and press a walnut half firmly onto each cake.
2 Bake for about 5 min at a temperature of 220–240°C, 425–475°F, Gas 9. Leave on a wire rack to cool.

Nougat Macaroons

1 quantity Macaroon Dough
about 200g (7oz) soft nougat
icing sugar, cocoa

1 Sprinkle icing sugar onto the work surface and roll out the dough to a thickness of about ½cm (¼in). Cut out squares measuring 4 × 4cm (1½ × 1½in).
2 Wrap a small piece of nougat inside each square and place the cakes with the joins facing down on a baking sheet lined with greaseproof paper.
Bake for 6–7 min at 220–240°C, 425–475°F, Gas 7–9. Decorate the cakes with piped glacé icing coloured with cocoa.

Nougat and Cherry Macaroons

These are made in the same way as the Macaroon Cakes with Nougat, but use cherries for decoration and spread icing over.

Napoleon's Hats

200g (7oz) butter
250 (9oz) plain flour
100g (¼lb) icing sugar, 2 egg yolks
½ quantity Macaroon Dough
glacé icing with cocoa added

1 Using both hands, rub the butter and the flour between fingertips and mix with icing sugar. Knead dough quickly to incorporate the egg yolks and put in a cool place for 1 hr.
2 Roll out and cut out round cakes about 4cm (1½in) in diameter. Place a small ball of macaroon dough on top and shape the pastry around.
3 Place cakes on greased baking sheet and bake for 6–8 min at 220°C, 425°F, Gas 7. Leave to cool on a wire rack. Decorate with icing.

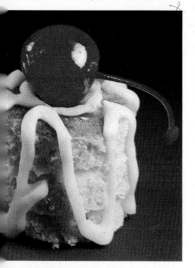

Petit Fours with Cherries

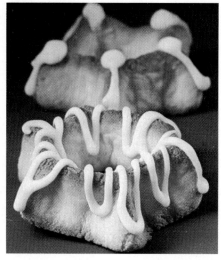

Macaroon Rings

Nougat Macaroons

Chocolate Petit Fours

Little Macaroon Cakes

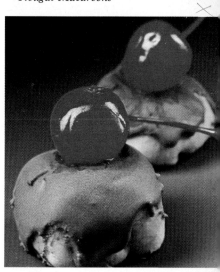

Nougat and Cherry Macaroons

Apricot Petit Fours

Fork Cakes

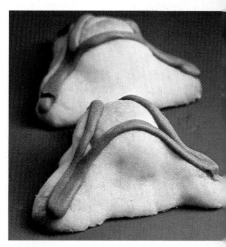

Napoleon's Hats

43

Rich Shortcrust Pastry

200–225g (7–8oz) butter
1–2 × 15ml tbsp (1–2tbsp) sugar
250g (9oz) plain flour
*2–3 × 15ml tbsp (2–3tbsp) cold
    water OR 1 large egg OR 2 egg
    yolks*
*25–50g (1–2oz) blanched almonds,
    ground or finely chopped*

Make the shortcrust pastry as explained in the illustrations and leave to rest for at least ½ hr.

Baked Pears
Preparation time: 15 min
Resting time for dough: ½–1 hr
Baking time: 10–15 min
Oven temperature: 200°C, 400°F, Gas 6
Unbaked pastry can be frozen

1 quantity Rich Shortcrust Pastry
Filling: 8 canned pears cut in half
apricot jam
1 egg for brushing

1 Roll out the dough to a fairly thin rectangle and cut out 16 rounds.
2 Brush half the rounds with apricot jam. Place well-drained pears in the middle and put the remaining rounds on top. Squeeze edges tightly together and place the rounds on a well-greased baking sheet. Brush with lightly whisked egg and bake as directed.
This quantity of shortcrust pastry can also be used to make a tart with a lid or with pastry placed in a criss-cross pattern on top. Use a 22cm (8½in) diameter flan tin.

Shortcrust Pastry

1 With both hands rub the chilled butter into the flour using fingertips.

2 Stir in sugar and add cold water, egg or egg yolks.

3 Collect dough loosely together with a rubber spatula or knife.

4 Knead dough quickly and lightly to give a smooth, firm consistency.

5 Place rolled out dough in a greased flan ring dusted with flour.

6 Press dough firmly onto the base and up the side.

7 Work the rolling pin across ring to cut off excess dough. Prick base well.

Juicy Berries

*Sun-ripened berries freshly
picked taste delicious as cake
fillings.
Blackcurrants and blueberries
are rich in both vitamins and
minerals and also extremely
tasty. Why not try them?*

Blackcurrant Rum Cake
Preparation time: 30 min
Baking time: Soft Sponge with Fat
(page 6)
Unsuitable for the freezer

*1 quantity Soft Sponge with Fat
about 225g (½lb) blackcurrants or
 blueberries
sugar, 2–3 × 15ml tbsp (2–3tbsp)
 rum*

*½ quantity Confectioner's Custard
 (see Chocolate Cake, page 14)
100–200ml (4–7fl oz) double cream
 or sour cream*

1 Sprinkle cleaned berries with
sugar to taste, sprinkle with rum and
leave to soak while baking the cake.
2 Bake cake in a greased spring-
form tin dusted with flour.
3 Turn the cake out carefully from
the tin and sprinkle with the juice
from the berries. Leave to cool on a
wire rack.
4 Cover cake with a layer of Confectioner's Custard and place berries
on top. Whip the cream and pipe
around the edge.

VARIATION
Make pastry as described on page
45. Line a flan ring, prick the base
well and bake for 10 min at 220°C,
425°F, Gas 7. Mix blackcurrants or
blueberries with 2–3 × 15ml tbsp
(2–3tbsp) sugar and 1 × 15ml tbsp
(1tbsp) of cornflour and place on top
of the pastry base. Bake for a further
10 min or so and leave to cool before
decorating with whipped double
cream or sour cream.

Tips for Busy People
Sprinkle a little rum on a ready-
made sponge-flan base available in
the shops, and place a layer of Confectioner's Custard (see Chocolate
Cake, page 14) on top. Alternatively
use either cream made from an egg
yolk mixed with sugar and whisked
until stiff then mixed with whipped
cream, or bought cream topping.
Cover with blackcurrant or blue-
berry jam or fresh berries sprinkled
with a dash of sugar, and decorate
the edge with whipped cream.

Crumble Cake with Peaches and Berries

Preparation time: 20 min
Baking time: 20–30 min
Oven temperature: 200°C, 400°F, Gas 6
Bottom of the oven
Can be frozen but will lose flavour

1 small quantity Shortcrust Pastry (see page 7)
3–4 ripe peaches, sugar
about 225g (½lb) blueberries, blackcurrants or other berries
2 × 15ml tbsp (2tbsp) cornflour
Crumble :
3 × 15ml tbsp (3tbsp) butter
6 × 15ml tbsp (6tbsp) sugar
6 × 15ml tbsp (6tbsp) flour
½ × 5ml tsp (½tsp) cinnamon, icing sugar

1 Roll out the shortcrust pastry and place in a well-greased tin or an ovenproof dish. Prick the base well with a fork and bake for 10–12 min in the middle of the oven. Leave to cool a little.

2 Peel fresh peaches, remove stones and cut fruit in slices. Sprinkle these with sugar and place in a dish. Cover the dish with tinfoil, place in the oven and allow the fruit to steam in its own juices for about 10 min. Pour off the juice.

3 Sprinkle the slightly cooled pastry base with 1 × 15ml tbsp (1tbsp) cornflour mixed with 2 × 15ml tbsp (2tbsp) sugar. Place well-drained peaches on top and arrange over them the well-drained berries mixed with 1 × 15ml tbsp (1tbsp) cornflour and sugar to taste. The cornflour will draw some of the liquid from the berries, which would otherwise have made the base soft.

4 Mix the ingredients for the crumble (except the icing sugar) and sprinkle on top of the berries. Bake for 15–20 min in the bottom of the oven until the crumble mixture is soft. Dust crumble with icing sugar when cold.

VARIATION
● The season for peaches is relatively short, and they can also be expensive to buy. Exchange fresh ones for well-drained peaches from a can. Do not steam these in the oven; they are ready for use.

● In place of blackcurrants or blueberries you can use redcurrants, firm stoned cherries or other berries. Strawberries or raspberries are not suitable as they contain too much moisture.

● Mix 25g (1oz) blanched, chopped almonds into the crumble mixture.

Versatile Pastry

Filled pastry bases are the answer for the housewife pressed for time.

Pastry bases, whether for tarts, flans or pies, provide the basis for a wide variety of sweets. Bake a few one day when you are not too busy and put them in the freezer. They are handy to have for the unexpected guest – they take only about ½ hr to defrost and uncooked fillings make completion a matter of minutes. But if you have a little more time, and don't rely on the freezer, the possibilities are endless, as the following recipes show.

Peach Tart from Italy (right)
Preparation time: 20 min
Baking time: see Shortcrust Pastry (page 7)
Unsuitable for the freezer

1 small quantity Shortcrust Pastry (page 7)
1 quantity Confectioner's Custard (see Chocolate Cake, page 14)
1 × 450g (1lb) can peaches

1 Place rolled out pastry in a pie dish sprinkled with flour. You can also use a spring-form tin. Press the pastry tightly against the side and, using the back of a knife, make a broad pattern along the rim.

2 Prick the base well with a fork or fill with tinfoil and dried beans. (Follow the instructions in the small illustrations below.) Bake the base at 200–220°C, 400–425°F, Gas 6–7. To give the tart a shiny edge, brush it with egg yolk or syrup from the can of fruit. Leave to cool.

3 Make the Confectioner's Custard and spoon into the base, arranging the drained peaches on top. Add a little syrup from the can of peaches if you like.

VARIATION
Instead of the Confectioner's Custard fill the cake with a peach mousse. Set aside some of the best-looking peach slices for decoration and mash the rest in a blender or press through a sieve. Add lemon juice or sherry to taste. Melt 15g (½oz) gelatine in 100ml (4fl oz) heated syrup from the peaches and pour this in a thin trickle into the fruit purée, while stirring vigorously. Pour the mousse into the pastry base and set aside to cool. Decorate with peaches and a few whirls of cream before serving.

Rhubarb Tart
Preparation time: 20 min
Baking time: see Shortcrust Pastry (page 7)
Unsuitable for the freezer

1 large quantity Shortcrust Pastry (see page 7)
about 450g (1lb) rhubarb

sugar
½–1 × 15ml tbsp (½–1tbsp) cornflour
1 egg yolk for brushing
about 200ml (7fl oz) double cream

1 Roll out about two-thirds of the pastry to a rectangle and place it in a greased flan tin dusted with flour. Either fill or prick the base (see illustrations), and bake for 10–12 min at 200°C, 400°F, Gas 6.
2 Sprinkle cleaned, sliced rhubarb pieces with sugar to taste. Leave mixture to boil until mushy on low heat. Thicken with cornflour stirred into 1 × 15ml tbsp (1tbsp) cold water. Or put the rhubarb pieces, covered and dusted with sugar and cornflour, in the oven, while tart base is baking.
3 Roll out the remaining pastry and cut into strips using a pastry wheel. Spoon the rhubarb into the base and arrange strips of dough on top in a criss-cross pattern. Brush with egg yolk and bake for a further 8–10 min at 220°C, 425°F, Gas 7. Serve warm, or cool and decorate with whipped cream.

VARIATION
Bake a flan base, using small quantity of Shortcrust Pastry (see page 7). Fill with rhubarb purée mixed with 50–100g (2–4oz) blanched, coarsely chopped almonds. Decorate with whipped cream or serve cream separately, or serve it with ice cream. Gooseberry purée could be used instead of rhubarb.

Tart Base from Shortcrust Pastry

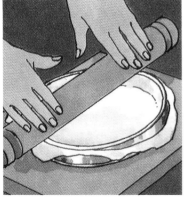

1 Place the rolled out pastry in a well-greased spring-form or flan tin, dusted with flour or breadcrumbs, allowing the pastry to hang over the rim. Trim with a rolling pin.

2 Collect the excess pastry and shape into a lump. Use this to press the pastry into the flan tin. Press the pastry well into the side.

3 Prick the pastry, or place crumpled tinfoil in the tin and fill with dried beans. This will prevent the pastry from rising.

Shiny and Decorative

Jellies and glazes give flans a decorative finish – exactly right for anyone with a special liking for these confections.

Glazed Grape Flan
Preparation time: about 30 min
Baking time: about 20 min
Unsuitable for the freezer

1 small quantity Shortcrust Pastry
  (see page 7)
½ quantity Confectioner's Custard
  (see Chocolate Cake, page 14)
about 300g (11oz) grapes
Glaze: 175g (6oz) sugar
100ml (4fl oz) water
2 × 15ml tbsp (2tbsp) vinegar

1 Roll out pastry to line a greased flan ring or spring-form baking tin, sprinkled with flour. Prick or fill the base as shown on page 48 and bake until cooked (about 20 min at 200–220°C, 400–425°F, Gas 6–7).
2 Make the Confectioner's Custard and, if liked, add a dash of sweet white wine. Spread cream evenly in the cooled base. Rinse the grapes, dry well and place on top of the cream.
3 Bring sugar and water to the boil, skim and stir in vinegar. Simmer until golden and smooth. Test if the glaze is ready by dipping a wooden spoon into cold water and then into the glaze. If the glaze feels crumbly and can be peeled off in flakes, it is ready. It will set very quickly and must therefore be poured over the grapes the moment it is ready. Be careful, as liquid glaze is piping hot.

Glazed Fruit as Cake Decoration
Small, whole fruits like grapes, cherries, plums, redcurrants, small pears or apples, are ideally suited to glazing. The same applies to sliced, firm fruits which do not contain too much water. All fruits should be dry, or the glaze will not stick.
Make a glaze, following the same procedure as that used for Glazed

Nobody can refuse Glazed Grape Flan.

Give your Apricot Flan a fresh flavour by adding raspberry or apple jelly and coarsely chopped almonds.

Grape Flan (above). Keep it warm in a bowl placed in saucepan of boiling water.
Dip in two or three fruits at a time, then take them out with two forks and place on greaseproof paper or a greased baking sheet to dry.
Small choux pastries and other dry, small cakes can be glazed in the same manner, or simply dipped halfway into the glaze.

Apricot Flan with Jelly
Preparation time: 20 min
Baking time: about 20 min
Unsuitable for the freezer

1 small quantity Shortcrust Pastry
  (see page 7)
½ quantity Confectioner's Custard
  (see Chocolate Cake, page 14)
1 can of apricots
apple or redcurrant jelly
3–4 × 15ml tbsp (3–4tbsp) sliced almonds

1 Roll out pastry to line a greased flan ring sprinkled with flour. Prick or fill the base as shown on page 48 and bake until cooked (about 20 min at 200–210°C, 400–410°F, Gas 6–6½).
2 Make the custard and, if liked, add some of the juice from the apricots. Place the cream in the cooled base and place drained apricots on top.
3 Thin the jelly with a little of the apricot juice. Spoon over the apricots and sprinkle almonds on top. Serve with whipped cream, mixed with either egg yolks whipped stiff with sugar, or sour cream.

Quick Tip
Make up ¼ packet jelly of appropriate flavour using only 65ml (2½fl oz) of liquid. Allow the jelly to nearly set before pouring it over fresh or tinned fruit in a previously baked base.

Strawberry Flan

Preparation time: 20 min
Baking time: about 20 min
Unsuitable for the freezer

1 small quantity Shortcrust Pastry
  (see page 7)
1 quantity Confectioner's Custard
  (see Chocolate Cake, page 14)
100–200ml (4–7fl oz) double cream
about ½kg (1lb 2oz) strawberries
sugar to taste

1 Roll out pastry to line a greased
flan ring sprinkled with flour. Prick
or fill the base as shown on page 48
and bake until cooked (about 20 min
at 200–210°C, 400–410°F, Gas
6–6½).
2 Make the custard, and stir in the
double cream.
3 Rinse and hull the strawberries.
Leave them to drain and cut into
slices. Sprinkle with sugar to
taste. Place cream and strawberries
alternately.

*Use fresh strawberries when they are in season, but this flan will be just
as tasty if you use frozen berries.*

Fruit Flan

Preparation time: 20 min
Baking time: see recipe for Soft
Sponge with Fat (page 6)
Unsuitable for the freezer

1 quantity Soft Sponge with Fat
  (see page 6)
4–5 × 15ml tbsp (4–5tbsp) sweet
  white wine
1 portion Jelly with equal parts of
  white wine and orange juice (see
  page 28)
2–3 bananas, 2–3 mandarins
a few black or green grapes

1 Bake cake in a greased sponge-flan
tin or a spring-form baking tin
sprinkled with flour. Turn cake out
onto a wire rack to cool and sprinkle
with the sweet white wine.
2 Make the jelly, mixing in a dash of
lemon juice for a fresher flavour.

3 Slice bananas, divide mandarins into segments, halve grapes and remove pips. Place on the cake base forming an attractive pattern with the rounded side of the grapes upwards. Spoon the half-set jelly on top to cover all fruits. Leave in a cool place for 1–2 hr before serving.

Mazarin Flan
Preparation time: 30 min
Baking time: 25–30 min
Oven temperature: 200°C, 400°F, Gas 6
Middle of the oven
Suitable for the freezer

1 small portion Shortcrust Pastry
  (see page 7)
Filling: 150g (5oz) almonds
85g (3½oz) sugar, 2 eggs
200ml (7fl oz) cream
1 × 15ml tbsp (1tbsp) flour
Coating: 50g (2oz) chocolate

Colourful Fruit Flan has a delicious flavour – served with or without cream.

1 Roll out pastry to line a greased flan ring sprinkled with flour.
2 Blanch the almonds. Keep 10–15 aside and grind the rest in a grinder or blender (liquidizer). Whisk eggs and sugar together and mix in the ground almonds, flour and cream.
3 Spread the filling in the pastry base and bake as directed above. Leave in the tin for a little while before carefully removing the flan ring. Allow to get cold.
4 Melt the chocolate in a saucepan placed in a larger saucepan filled with hot water, or on very low heat. Brush over the cooled tart. Coarsely chop the 10–15 almonds and sprinkle on before the chocolate sets hard.

Gorgeous Pies

The pie is no newcomer to the cookery scene; it has a long tradition. Here we include two unusual ones.

Apple Pie (left)

Preparation time: 15–20 min
Baking time: see Shortcrust Pastry (page 7)
Suitable for the freezer, but will deteriorate somewhat in taste

1 large quantity Shortcrust Pastry (see page 7)
3–4 apples
4 × 15ml tbsp (4tbsp) sugar
2 × 5ml tsp (2tsp) cinnamon
60g (2½oz) raisins
1 × 15ml tbsp (1tbsp) grated lemon rind
1 egg

1 Line a greased pie dish with about two-thirds of the rolled out pastry. Prick the bottom well.
2 Peel, core and thinly slice the apples. Place them in the dish and sprinkle with a mixture of sugar, cinnamon, raisins and grated lemon rind.
3 Cut the remaining pastry into strips. Plait together in threes, or flute, and place lattice-fashion on top of the filling, pressing the edges firmly. Brush the pie with lightly whisked egg and bake as directed. Serve warm with cream or custard.

Pear and Plum Pie

Use the same procedure as for English Apple Pie, but fill with a mixture of 3–4 sliced pears, 8–10 stoned plums, 50g (2oz) chopped almonds, sugar to taste and 1 × 15ml tbsp (1tbsp) cornflour to bind together some of the fruit juice. Dust lightly with icing sugar when cooked.

Grape Pie

Bake a base, using a small quantity of Rich Shortcrust Pastry (see page 45). Roll out 100–200g (4–7oz) marzipan into a circle and place in the baked base. Fill with 225–350g (½–¾lb) grapes cut in half with pips removed. Make 1 quantity Jelly with sweet white wine and light fruit juice (see page 28), or use packet jelly. Pour the half-set jelly over the grapes and put the pie in a cool place until the jelly has set. Serve with or without whipped cream.

Two completely different pies. The Grape Pie with jelly is served cold, while the Pear and Plum Pie can be served warm.
Both can be served with whipped or sour cream.

Tempting Tortes with Fruit

Fruit and berries add a nice, fresh flavour. Use fresh ones when these are in season – the rest of the year we make do with either frozen or canned.

Square Apricot Torte (above)
Preparation time: 15 min
Baking time: see Shortcrust Pastry
(page 7)
Unsuitable for the freezer

1 small quantity Shortcrust Pastry
(see page 7)
1 × 450g (1lb) can of apricots
3–4 × 15ml tbsp (3–4tbsp) sugar
1–2 × ml tsp (1–2tsp) vanilla sugar
icing sugar

1 Roll out about two-thirds of the pastry and line a small Swiss roll tin or a shape made of greaseproof paper and placed on a baking sheet.
2 Place drained apricots, sprinkled with sugar mixed with vanilla sugar, on top. Crumble over the rest of the pastry and bake as directed.
Cool the torte and sprinkle with icing sugar before serving.

Gooseberry Torte with Meringue
Preparation time: 20 min
Baking time: see Shortcrust Pastry
(page 7)
Unsuitable for the freezer

1 small quantity Shortcrust Pastry
(see page 7)
about ½kg (1lb) fresh gooseberries
sugar, vanilla essence

Meringue:
3 egg whites
150g (5oz) sugar
½ × 5ml tsp (1tsp) vinegar

1 Make the pastry as described in the basic recipe and roll out to a rectangular shape. Use to line a greased flan tin sprinkled with flour. Prick the base well or fill as shown on page 48. Bake base for 10 min at 220°C, 425°F, Gas 7.
2 Boil the gooseberries until soft, but still whole, in sweetened water with vanilla essence added. Drain well.
3 Whisk egg whites with sugar and vinegar until stiff. Place the gooseberries in the pastry base and cover them with the meringue. Bake torte for further 15–20 min at 160–180°C, 325–350°F, Gas 3–4.

American Apricot Torte

Preparation time: 15 min
Baking time: see Shortcrust Pastry
  (page 7)
Suitable for the freezer

1 large quantity Shortcrust Pastry
  (page 7)
about 200ml (7fl oz) apricot purée
  or jam

1 Roll out about two-thirds of the pastry to a rectangular shape and line a greased flan tin sprinkled with flour. Prick bottom well.
2 Spread the apricot purée or jam evenly on the base and cover with a criss-cross pattern of rolled out pastry. Bake as directed.

Apricot Slices

The ingredients are the same as for American Apricot Torte, but the method is different. Roll out the pastry to a rectangle measuring about 30 × 40cm (12 × 16in). Cut into four equal lengths. Prick well and bake them for 15–20 min on a greased baking sheet or greaseproof paper at an oven temperature of 200°C, 400°F, Gas 6. Leave to cool. Place the lengths together in twos with apricot jam in between. Make a smooth icing of 100g (¼lb) icing sugar and about 1 × 15ml tbsp (1tbsp) orange juice.
Spread the icing over the cakes and, when hardened, cut into even-sized slices.

Spring Cake

Preparation time: 15–20 min
Baking time: about 1¼ hr
Oven temperature: 110–120°C,
225–250°F, Gas ¼–½
Middle of the oven
Unsuitable for the freezer

3 egg whites
150g (5oz) sugar
300–400ml (½–¾pt) double cream
1 × 5ml tsp (1tsp) instant coffee
1–2 × 5ml tsp (1–2tsp) cocoa
50–75g (2–3oz) plain chocolate,
  grated

1 Whisk egg whites until stiff, add
sugar, a little at a time, and whisk
until the meringue is stiff and can be
shaped into peaks.
2 Grease a baking sheet and
sprinkle with flour or line with
greaseproof paper. Make two circles
on the paper by drawing round a
plate. Divide the meringue evenly to
fill the circles.
3 With the oven door a little ajar,
bake the bases until they are dry and
can be removed from the greaseproof paper or the baking sheet.
Allow to cool.
4 Whip the cream and add instant
coffee and cocoa. Sandwich the
bases together with the flavoured
cream and sprinkle with grated
chocolate.
Serve the cake at once when it has
been filled and decorated, or the
meringue bases will go soft.

Russian Apple Torte (right)

Preparation time: 20 min
Baking time: see Shortcrust Pastry
(page 7)
Suitable for the freezer

1 large quantity Shortcrust Pastry
  (see page 7)
5–6 firm apples, 1 lemon
60g (2½oz) brown sugar
1 × 5ml tsp (1tsp) ginger
60g (2½oz) raisins
85g (3½oz) sugar
2 × 15ml tbsp (2tbsp) butter, 1 egg

Left : Whether you use dried, boiled
or chopped apricots, apricot purée or
jam, both American Apricot Torte
(above) and Apricot Slices are
delicious.

1 Roll out two-thirds of the shortcrust pastry to a rectangular shape
and line a greased flan tin sprinkled
with flour, or use a spring-form tin.
Prick the pastry base well.
2 Peel the apples, slice and place
about half of them in the tin. Mix
brown sugar, ginger and most of the
raisins, and place on top of the
apples.
3 Place the rest of the apples and
raisins on top, squeeze the lemon
and pour the juice over the apples.
Dot the butter over the top. Reserve
2–3 × 15ml tbsp (2–3tbsp) sugar
and sprinkle the rest over the fruit.
4 Roll out the remaining pastry for
a lid and cut out small leaf-shaped
holes. Brush the pastry rim with
lightly whisked egg and press the lid
firmly into place. Brush the top with
egg, sprinkle the remaining sugar
over and bake as directed.
Serve warm with or without whipped cream, or with a little sour
cream.

Torte with Jam and Sour Cream

Preparation time: 15 min
Baking time: see Shortcrust Pastry
(page 7)
Suitable for the freezer

1 large quantity Shortcrust Pastry
  (see page 7)
180–200g (6½–7oz) blanched
  almonds
3–4 × 15ml tbsp (3–4tbsp) raspberry
  jam
3–4 × 15ml tbsp (3–4tbsp) cherry
  jam
3–4 × 15ml tbsp (3–4tbsp) sour
  cream
1 × 5ml tsp (1tsp) cinnamon
1 egg yolk, 1 egg for brushing

1 Line a greased pie dish with two-
thirds of the shortcrust pastry and
prick well.
2 Grind the almonds and mix with
jams, sour cream, cinnamon and egg
yolk. Spread the filling evenly in the
dish.
3 Roll out the rest of the pastry.
Place on top of the filling as a lid
with holes cut in it, or cut out strips
and place over the top in a criss-
cross pattern.
Brush the pastry rim with a little
lightly whisked egg and press the lid
firmly into place. Brush the whole
surface with egg and sprinkle with a
little sugar. Bake as directed. Serve
warm or cold with, if you like, extra
sour cream and cinnamon.

Strudel

Strudel is an Austrian speciality. You need a good rolling pin for it, to get the dough as thin as possible. This way your strudel will be crisp and delicious – as in a first-class delicatessen.

Cherry Studel (left)
Preparation time: 30 min
Resting time: 30 min
Baking time: 40–50 min
Oven temperature: 180–200°C, 350–400°F, Gas 4–6
Middle of the oven
Unsuitable for the freezer

Pastry: 100g ($\frac{1}{4}$lb) flour
pinch of salt
2 × 15ml tbsp (2tbsp) tepid water
2 × 15ml tbsp (2tbsp) melted butter
1 × 15ml tbsp (1tbsp) oil for rolling out
Filling: about 400g (14oz) canned cherries, stoned
1 × 15ml tbsp (1tbsp) cornflour
75g (3oz) butter, melted
2 × 15ml tbsp (2tbsp) breadcrumbs
4 × 15ml tbsp (4tbsp) sugar
25g (1oz) almonds, icing sugar

1 Mix flour and salt into a bowl, make a well in the middle and add tepid water and melted butter alternately, while working flour into the liquid with the fingertips. Work the dough quickly until smooth.

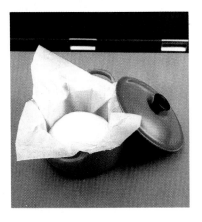

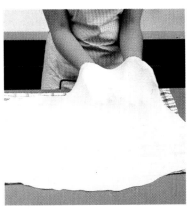

Strudel
1 Leave the dough to rest in a warm place in a preheated saucepan.

2 Roll out the dough thinly on a cloth sprinkled with flour, leaving the edges a little thicker. Stretch out carefully.

3 Place the filling on the dough and roll up by means of the cloth.

2 Rinse a saucepan with boiling water on the outside to make it warm, but dry inside. Wrap the dough in greaseproof paper, place it in the saucepan and put the lid on. Leave in a warm place for about 30 min.

3 Meanwhile make the filling. Stir the cornflour into 150ml (¼pt) cold syrup from the cherries, bring to the boil while stirring, and carefully fold in the drained cherries. Place the mixture in a cool place.

4 Place a large evenly woven piece of cloth on the table and sprinkle with flour. Roll out the dough on this until thin, but leave the edges a little thicker than the rest of the dough. Roll carefully to avoid any cracks or holes. Brush the rolled out dough with oil and stretch carefully, working from the centre outwards (see illustrations).

5 Spread 50g (2oz) butter, breadcrumbs, sugar and blanched, chopped almonds over two-thirds of the dough's surface, leaving a margin of about 3cm (1in) each side of the dough. Place the cherries on top and roll up the dough by means of the cloth. Squeeze the edges tightly together.

6 Place the cake carefully, with the joins facing downwards, on a baking sheet covered with greaseproof paper. Brush with some of the remaining 25g (1oz) butter and bake as directed brushing several times more during baking. Dust lightly with icing sugar when cool.

Apple Strudel is often served with cold custard.

Apple Strudel

This is made in the same way as Cherry Strudel, but is filled with about 1kg (2¼lb) peeled and sliced apples. Place butter, breadcrumbs, sugar and chopped almonds on the dough as in the previous recipe. Place the apples sprinkled with 2 × 15ml tbsp (2tbsp) sugar, 1 × 5ml tsp (1tsp) cinnamon and 90g (¼lb) raisins on top. Roll up, brush and bake as for Cherry Strudel. Sprinkle with icing sugar when cold and serve with custard.

Marzipan Torte with Fruit
Preparation time: 20 min
Baking time: 12–14 min
Oven temperature: 220–230°C,
425–450°F, Gas 7–8
Middle of the oven
Suitable for the freezer without the
filling

Base : 1 quantity Soft Macaroon
Dough (see Easy-to-make
Macaroon, page 42)
butter
Filling : 4 slices canned pineapple
1 × 450g (1lb) can peaches or
apricots, ½ lemon
15g (½oz) powdered gelatine

1 Make the macaroon dough.
2 Draw a circle about 24–26cm (9½–10½in) in diameter on grease-proof paper and brush with a little melted butter. Spread about a half of the dough evenly within the circle.
3 Spoon the remaining dough into a piping bag with a star nozzle and make 4 stripes crossed diagonally over the base, so that you have 8 triangular areas. Pipe the rest of the dough around the edge.
4 Bake the cake until lightly golden, and cool on a plate before removing the greaseproof paper with a palette knife.
5 Soak the gelatine in cold water for

about 10 min and melt with 100ml (4fl oz) of heated juice from the fruit. Stir in the juice of ½ lemon and 150ml (¼pt) cold fruit juice.
6 Cut the well-drained fruit into slices and place them so that they form a pattern on the cake base. Pour the half-set jelly over.
Serve the cake well chilled, as it is or with lightly whipped cream or custard.
The baked base can be frozen, and filled with fruit and jelly when defrosted.
The completed cake will keep for a few days if well wrapped in plastic film.

Homemade Marzipan Torte tastes delicious and looks as good as it tastes.

Peach Turnovers

9 cakes
Preparation time: 15 min
Baking time: 12–15 min
Oven temperature: 220°C, 425°F, Gas 7
Middle of the oven
Unsuitable for the freezer

¾ quantity Puff Pastry (see page 7)
100g (¼lb) marzipan
1 × 450g (1lb) can halved peaches
1 egg for brushing
2 × 15ml tbsp (2tbsp) apricot jam
25g (1oz) almonds

1 Roll out the pastry (you can buy ready-made frozen pastry and defrost) to a square about 30 × 30cm (12 × 12in) and slice into nine squares measuring 10 × 10cm (about 4 × 4in).
2 Place a piece of marzipan and a half, well-drained peach on each square. Gather up the corners and squeeze tightly around the peaches. You can use another scrap of dough on top to make the join really tight. Brush with lightly whisked egg.
3 Bake as directed. Brush the warm turnovers with apricot jam and sprinkle with a few toasted flaked almonds. Lightly boiled apples can be used instead of peaches.

Peach Turnovers have been brushed with apricot jam. This, along with the almonds, adds a nice flavour.

Index